"By condensing complic
a bite-sized book, Jeff
produced a valuable introduction
understand China, he has also distilled issues to their crux. In so doing, the book holds punchy insights on Chinese politics and history that even seasoned China-watchers should find rewarding."

CINDY YU
The Times (London)

"Jeffrey Wasserstrom's latest book is readable, enjoyable, and quotable. It has much to offer China savvy folk as well as casual readers."

DAVID MOSER
Author of A Billion Voices: China's Search for a Common Language

"Jeffrey Wasserstrom excels at turning his deep knowledge of China into accessible, entertaining reading for the uninitiated. Everything You Wanted to Know About China is a lively introduction to key aspects of the country today."

TANIA BRANIGAN
The Guardian

"Among the thousands of books and articles about China available today, Wasserstrom's concise primer is an invaluable resource. From Confucius through Mao to Xi Jinping, it tells you the essentials of what we know—and do not know—about the Middle Kingdom."

VICTOR MALLET
Financial Times

First published in 2025 by Bui Jones Books

Front cover illustration and book design by Katie Murphy

BUI JONES

Printed and bound in Great Britain by Clays Ltd Elcograf S.p.A.
A CIP catalogue record for this book is available from the British Library

ISBN 978-1-0685257-9-7

Everything you wanted to know about China*

* But were afraid to ask

Contents

Foreword

We need to start with the swinger scene in Nixon-era New York. Yes, really. Not because the biggest news story early in 1972 in that city and around the world was Nixon's trip to Beijing to meet Mao, but because this book takes its title from a Woody Allen film that was a big hit that same year: *Everything You Always Wanted to Know about Sex* (*But Were Afraid to Ask)*.

Jeffrey Wasserstrom has taken on a subject perhaps as sensitive, though less taboo, than the one parodied by Woody Allen. Knowing about modern China is an essential part of understanding the world today. Perhaps as recently as the early 1990s one might have argued that China was large but essentially in the background when it came to changing the world. No longer. With the second biggest population in the world after India, the second biggest economy and the second biggest military after the United States, China's size is now matched by its significance.

Yet it remains a hard place for outsiders to interpret easily. As China has globalized over time, its elites and its emergent middle class have become increasingly familiar with the western world. But the reverse has not become the case. Of course, many people have indeed become familiar with particular aspects of China: those involved with US security are very aware of the country's military capacities; advocates of European business understand its centrality to supply chains and the size of its market; and consumers in Africa and Latin America have become aware of its technological capacities as they touch the screen of their Chinese-made smartphones. But the bigger picture still remains elusive.

This book does sterling work in posing—and answering—questions that show that one should not just concentrate on the endless headlines about China, but instead understand the wider framing that shapes the country and its relationship with the world. Wasserstrom is a distinguished historian, and his understanding of the past is one of the factors that distinguishes this particular interpretation of China. In China, perhaps more than any other major society, an understanding of the past is vital to reading the present.

This is particularly true in the 2020s, when China seems to be in the midst of a debate about its own identity. China is a state run by a Marxist-Leninist party but which also draws explicitly on the legacy of Confucius, a thinker dedicated to ideas of order and hierarchy rather than revolutionary change. The contradictions inherent in that political ecology were graphically illustrated in 2023 when a Chinese television station broadcast the show *When Confucius Met Marx*, a five-part conversation between two actors representing the two thinkers, exploring how far their two systems of thought might be compatible with China's contemporary reality. For decades now in China, there have been rehabilitations of Confucius's life and thought, adapted for a contemporary audience. There has also been a new revival of interest in Marxism, with new institutes analysing its significance popping up in various universities. This debate has been given further urgency by the rapid changes in global policy that the second Trump administration has initiated. China sees opportunities as well as risks in the new world, and as it thinks about worldviews, it reverts frequently to interpretations of the past, and the legacy of its own philosophical systems.

One of the most interesting subjects examined in Wasserstrom's account of China is the dynamic between technology, control and freedom. He writes with understanding and not a little irony about the way in which censorship in China is both comprehensive and full of holes. Open dissidence is censored, but books with hugely relevant messages for authoritarian societies such as George Orwell's *Nineteen Eighty-Four*, are not. He also writes about the unpredictability of China's political ecology, pointing out that uncertainty is part of the point: if you are not sure what the results of your action will be, you may decide simply not to act at all.

Yet the world China is helping to create may no longer allow the simple passivity of non-action. At the time of writing, China is in a contradictory position, generating huge amounts of technological innovation yet unable to create sufficient jobs to employ young people, who are showing signs of disillusionment with a political and social model that seems to offer them only a pressured and financially precarious lifestyle. (Not dissimilar, perhaps, from the west.) It is restless, trying to solve its own problems in ways that inevitably have consequences for the rest of us. China is also becoming one of the most important actors in global politics. Its preferences already shape key UN institutions including the Human Rights Council, where it stresses economic well being over civil liberties, and UNESCO, from which the US recently pulled out, and which will likely be influenced by new Chinese ideas such as the still vaguely defined Global Civilizational Initiative. And in the spheres of artificial intelligence, energy transition and critical mineral supply, China is already a key actor and will be a large part of the conversation about shaping norms and rules in the 2030s and beyond.

Global changes will take place under immense amounts of Chinese influence. Yet understanding how China works, and how its past is likely to shape not just its own future, but all of our futures—this is a work in progress, and a task that not nearly enough people are undertaking. We're fortunate to have Wasserstrom's decades of scholarship, curiosity, and principle to help us on the journey. Sometimes it can indeed seem intimidating to know where to start when it comes to understanding China. If you were afraid to ask—fear not. You have come to the right book.

Rana Mitter
Harvard Kennedy School
November 2025

HISTORY
&
IDEOLOGY

Xi Jinping and Mao Zedong

What are the parallels between Xi and Mao? What do they have in common?

The biggest commonality between them is that they're both the subjects of personality cults. Mao was the centre of an intense personality cult from 1949 to 1976. And when he died, on 9 September 1976, there was tremendous outpouring of grief, even among people who had suffered immensely from his policies. Xi Jinping is the first Chinese leader since Mao who has had a sustained personality cult of the kind where if you walk into a bookshop in China, the first things you see are books by him, which are more or less collections of his speeches. When Mao was alive, you might've thought that's sort of what happened with Communist Party leaders in China. But after

Mao's death, there was an aversion to that kind of personality cult. One sign of this was not publishing the speeches of leaders until they were dead or had stepped down from the top spots.

I first travelled to China in the middle of 1986 at a time when Deng Xiaoping was the most powerful person in the country. In the entire year I spent there doing doctoral research, I don't recall ever seeing a book that celebrated Deng or was made up of his speeches. Having spent a lot of time studying the Mao era, I was surprised by the relative lack of these signs of a personality cult. You could go for days then without being aware of who was in charge. I only occasionally saw posters in public places or photographs in homes featuring Deng—a break from the omnipresence of those sorts of things featuring Mao in an earlier time. Everyone knew that, despite not holding a formal top title like "Chairman" or "Premier", Deng was the most powerful person in China. They also knew he was the country's first major leader since Mao, as Hua Guofeng, Mao's immediate successor, spent just a couple of years at the top before being pushed aside. There were few Deng posters, though, and the newspapers referred to him plenty but weren't dominated by stories about him. He was quoted, but his words weren't treated as sacred. With Xi Jinping, you've had a throwback to an earlier period in Communist Party rule, which seemed as though it might be completely relegated to the past. Posters showing Xi are commonplace. In bookstores, there are tomes on "Xi Jinping Thought", hagiographic accounts of the leader's life, collections of his speeches.

The ubiquity of Xi's face and words in today's China is a notable throwback to Mao's day, but a key difference between the two leaders is that only the long-dead one revelled in chaos and class struggle. Tellingly, Mao's favourite work of Chinese fiction was *Journey to the West*, whose central figure, Sun Wukong (also known as the Monkey King), was a classic agent of chaos. In that novel, published in the 16th century, the Monkey King could turn the heavens upside down and make mischief of all kinds. Like the Monkey King, Mao embraced disorder and the potential benefits of upending all hierarchies—all those, that is, aside from his own high position. He often talked about class struggle and wrote a lot about the revolutionary masses battling and toppling elite groups, ideas he drew from Marxism. But unlike Marx, Mao thought that in China, which was still mostly rural and agricultural, the vast ranks of the peasantry as well as the smaller set of industrial workers were both crucial revolutionary classes. Mao stressed revolutionary spirit above all else, often calling for new bouts of class struggle to shake things up and keep everyone off guard.

By contrast, Xi, unlike his predecessor Mao, is obsessed with maintaining order. He prizes stability and predictability. Also, while Xi says he's a Marxist, he does not emphasise at all the class struggle side of Marxism. Mao liked to stir things up via mass movements, and he was drawn to the spectacle of people on the streets clamouring for change. Xi, on the other hand, doesn't like the idea of people taking to the streets in any form that can't be controlled. So grand parades are part of the Xi era, but ecstatic rallies like the marches Red Guard loyalists held for Mao are not.

Xi's obsession with order, where does it come from?

Confucius. While Mao never talked positively about Confucius or claimed China's Confucian traditions were worth extolling, Xi does those things. Confucianism has many strands, but it is mainly a school of thought based on calling for stable hierarchies and veneration of tradition. In other words, it is the opposite of a Monkey King approach to the world, though both approaches deserve to be seen as "Chinese" through and through. In an ideal Confucian society, there are clear and enduring categories of superior and inferior, with both parties owing something to the other: the former owing the latter care, the latter owing the former respect and deference. Mao viewed all tradition-based hierarchies with suspicion. He thought of Confucianism as a feudal form of thought that had held China back. Xi likes to quote Confucius, but Red Guards wanted to destroy all relics associated with Confucius and his clan in Qufu, where the sage was from, and where rituals honouring the ancient philosopher on his birthday are now held.

Mao and Xi are clearly similar in how effective both have been at concentrating their political power, and the fact that Xi praises Mao and many call Xi the most powerful leader since Mao reinforces this idea. But in their attitudes toward class struggle and mass movements they're different, even opposites. Despite this contrast, both leaders clearly share one goal: to see China stay under the rule of the Chinese Communist Party and to see its status in the world rise.

The Civil War

How did Mao end up ruling China? Was there a war?

The easy way to answer this is to say his forces beat the Nationalist Party, headed by his arch-rival Chiang Kai-shek, in a civil war that began after the Second World War ended. But the road that brought Mao to power in 1949 at the close of the Civil War had many twists and turns.

We need to first say that China was under the rule of emperors until 1912. The monarchical system was overthrown by an upheaval, known as the 1911 Revolution, that was carried out partly by people who wanted to change China into a republic and partly by people who wanted to get rid of the imperial rulers in power at the time. That ruling family was known as the Qing. Some of the revolutionaries saw the Qing as illegitimate, made up of outsiders from the far northeast, nomads of the steppes. The Qing emperors, the first of whom took power when his armies swept down from north of the Great Wall and conquered China in 1644, were ethnically Manchu, not Han, the majority group in many territories south of the Great Wall. Some anti-Qing insurgents didn't mind emperors, they just wanted them to be ethnically Chinese—that is, Han. It was a strange combination. There were ethnic nationalists who wanted China back under the control of Han. There were people who thought the time for rule by emperors was over and wanted to establish a republic. They joined together in October 1911 to rise up. And then on the first day of 1912 Sun Yat-sen was proclaimed the provisional president of a newly formed Republic of China. But then he got nudged out of power by Yuan Shikai, a military strongman who was ethnically Chinese but had served the Qing before switching sides to oppose the imperial family. After Yuan's death, there was a period where the country was divided between competing warlords who each controlled small bits of territory.

The Republic of China didn't have a strong government and was essentially ruled by these military strongmen. There were then two groups that emerged to oppose them. One rallied around Sun Yat-sen, who had founded something that became known as the Nationalist Party. And then, there was a small group of people who formed a communist party. Mao was one of them. The members of this group were intellectuals, most of them young, who had taken part in a 1919 struggle called the May Fourth Movement, which was named for the day of a student protest that called for an end to autocratic strongman rule and to imperialists bullying China.

Mao and the other founders of the Chinese Communist Party were inspired by Marxist ideas, but they were also just excited by the Russian Revolution. Russia was nearby. What happened there seemed relevant to Chinese intellectuals trying to figure out how to change China for the better. Russia had a largely rural population, just like China, and somehow it seemed to be getting strong in the world. And there was an interest in how China could do that.

So the Soviet Union was important to China's communist movement?

Yes. The newly formed Soviet Union did something on the diplomatic front that was very important to Chinese patriots of all political stripes. They renounced the concessions that the Qing had been bullied into giving the tsars around the turn of the century.

The backdrop for this was the Boxer Uprising. It began with anti-Christian North China peasants who used martial arts and thought they could call down spirit soldiers to aid them in attacking Chinese Protestants and Catholics and foreign missionaries. It ended with the Boxers, backed by the Qing, laying siege to Beijing in the summer of 1900, threatening the lives of diplomats and their families. The siege ended when an international force of soldiers from eight countries, including Russia, stormed the capital and freed the hostages. Since the Qing had supported the Boxers, they were forced to make amends for the uprising by paying a large indemnity to the foreign powers.

After the Russian Revolution in 1917, the newly formed Soviet Union renounced all the special privileges Tsarist Russia had gained from being part of the forces from the West and Japan that had defeated the Boxers. The new communist rulers in Moscow said that the settlement imposed on the Qing was an unfair benefit gained at the expense of a weaker country. That it was imperialism, and they wanted nothing to do with it. One important idea that Lenin, leader of the Russian Revolution, added to Marxism was that imperialist powers repressed other countries in a way that was analogous to how elite classes repressed the working classes. And so, while Marx's ideas of class struggle were attractive to some of the activists who had taken part in the May Fourth Movement, the founders of China's Communist Party were especially drawn to Lenin's vision. They liked his combined emphasis on anti-imperialism and the need for a vanguard party to lead a country forward, a second important part of the Leninist half of Marxism-Leninism.

When the struggle against warlord rule grew intense in the early-to-mid-1920s, the Communist Party was small, much smaller than the Nationalist

Party. The two organizations worked together for a time because Sun Yat-sen wanted them to put their difference aside until the country was unified and no longer run by corrupt military strongmen. Even though he wasn't a Marxist, Sun admired Lenin and Leninism, just as Mao and Mao's comrades did. This made it easy to him to feel that, while the Communist and the Nationalist parties had different views on the path forward for China, they had important things in common. Most importantly, they agreed on who the enemies were—the warlords and grasping foreign powers. The problem came when Sun died in 1925, and Chiang Kai-shek, his brother-in-law, took over the Nationalist Party.

Chiang initially kept the alliance going, but in 1927 he turned against the Communists and tried to destroy them—and almost succeeded. His armies defeated the warlords and by 1928 his Nationalist Party ruled the country. The Communist Party, on the other hand, was reduced to small groups on the run, setting up base in different parts of the country. They were pursued by Chiang's armies and when captured were either imprisoned or killed. Chiang and his allies claimed to be carrying on Sun's legacy and referred to the Communists as "red bandits" and "counter-revolutionaries". The Communists countered by claiming that *they* were carrying on Sun's legacy and were trying to get the revolution back on track. Chiang, they claimed, was just another warlord.

In 1928, if you'd boldly predicted that the

Communist Party would end up victorious 21 years later with someone named Mao in charge of a newly formed country, people in China would have laughed at you. Most would have had no idea who the Communists were. Those who *did* know would not have known who Mao was. And most of those who knew about the Communists and about Mao would have viewed them as being no match for the much better funded and better armed Nationalist Party and him as no match for Chiang.

The Rise of Mao

How did Mao get on top? How did he come to power?

There's a compelling official story to tell about how all this happened, which has been told and retold in all sorts of media in China since 1949. It is repeated in textbooks, of course. It was also the basis for a lavish song and dance musical called *The East is Red*, which was staged and filmed in 1964. In that spectacle and in television shows, audience saw actors playing dashing Red Army soldiers battle villainous Nationalist and Japanese troops trying to kill them and harm ordinary Chinese people. It is a story that is partly true. There really was a Long March (1934-1935), an event that is elevated to the status of sacred quest in Communist lore. Red Army soldiers did play a role in defeating Japan and then bested Nationalist ones in battle. But it is a story partly based on exaggerations and distortions.

At its heart, the story conforms to the approach of Great Man history while mixing in David vs. Goliath elements. Mao is the Great Man. He is credited with having had a couple of big ideas. One was that peasants could be a revolutionary force, and the other was that guerrilla warfare strategies could defeat a much stronger military force by using unconventional tactics. The David vs. Goliath part comes in via the idea that a ragtag group of Communists on the run kept evading the Nationalist Party, eventually moving across thousands of miles of treacherous terrain on an extended trek that resulted in them being able to regroup in isolated mountain base areas beyond the reach of Chiang Kai-shek's forces. The tale of the Great Man and the ragtag group ends with a temporary second alliance with the Nationalist Party from 1937 to 1945 to fight together against Japanese invaders and then a civil war that the Communists win. This, so the tale goes, sometimes told in a breathless manner that reminds me of accounts of the heroes of *The Lord of the Rings* overcoming obstacle after obstacle, ended in a "liberation" welcomed by all the people of China.

The factors that led to the Communist triumph, in this official mythic version of the past, included Mao having better ideas than Chiang and being progressive while his foe was traditionalistic, but other things are brought up too. Ordinary people backed the Communists over the Nationalists, it's said, because they were less corrupt, treated peasants and workers better, and were seen as having done more to fight the

Japanese. The Nationalists supposedly never gave up on the idea of trying to exterminate the Communists and let this divert their attention from battling the true enemy—imperial Japan. And they were not true patriots, despite being called the "Nationalists", the story goes, since they talked about freeing China from foreign control but were bankrolled by and in league with the American imperialists.

A lot of this has at least a kernel of truth. What it leaves out is that not all Chinese people welcomed the Communist victory. Chiang's forces, as some Chinese official accounts now acknowledge, played a role in defeating Japan. While Chiang was obsessed with defeating the Communists, he also saw the importance of fighting the foreign invaders. It is also important that, while the Nationalists benefited from US support, the Communists got support from the Soviet Union. There is also a lot that gets swept under the rug about intense infighting among the Communist Party leadership, and other unsavoury things like opium being grown in base areas and sales of it helping to support the Party.

So there are quite a few similarities between Mao and Chiang?

One thing that set Chiang and Mao clearly apart was that the former praised Confucius and saw no problem with working with heads of companies and bankers, while the latter talked of freeing China from the hold of feudal Confucian ideas and doing away with all vestiges of capitalism. As much as Xi talks about carrying forward the legacy of 1949, sometimes he gives speeches that bring up themes that Mao would not recognize as the words of Chinese Communist Party leader. If Chiang were to come back to life, on the other hand, that *Nationalist Party* leader might think Xi sounded like one *his* successors, not a successor to his arch-rival.

Interestingly, there are parallels between Chiang and Xi, the current leader. Chiang had, like Xi has, a high-profile wife who was a celebrity figure in her day and was known around the world. Both were more like first ladies than Mao's wife ever was. Also, Chiang and Xi oversaw periods of emphasising more traditional patriarchal values in China. Mao had many flaws—he did some terrible things at the interpersonal level, including destroying factional enemies, and at the policy level, like launching campaigns that took a terrible toll in lives lost—but he promoted the need for greater equality between the sexes. There were good moves toward giving girls and women more educational opportunities. The Marriage Law of 1950 was introduced that gave men and women a more equal legal position than they had ever had. Since his death, the Chinese Communist Party has paid less attention to promoting gender equality. And especially since Xi's rise, it has promoted the idea that women should play traditional roles, which is more in step with Chiang's Taiwan than Mao's China.

Ironically, in post-Chiang Taiwan, over a long period with its own complex history of democratisation, we reached a point recently where a woman was elected president. That was the first time in any part of Asia, at least in recent times, when a woman who had no ties by blood or marriage to a past male leader reached the top spot in a government. In the 1950s and 1960s, Mao talked about women "holding up half the sky". Chiang, by contrast, promoted traditional Confucian family values. If asked a group of politically minded gamblers to bet on whether Taiwan or the mainland would get a female leader first, they would have surely said smart money would have been on the People's Republic of China. Of course, back then, if you were asked to bet on whether a Taiwan city or mainland one would someday be the site of a major spectacle in which Confucius was quoted and actors took the stage portraying his disciples in a positive way, the smart money would have been on Taipei. Yet when those two things happened, it was in Beijing's Bird's Nest Stadium at the start of the 2008 Olympics. The history of China, like that of other parts of the world, is full of surprises.

The Great Leap Forward

Some 30 to 45 million died in the Great Leap Forward, making it one of the greatest atrocities in human history. How did this catastrophe unfold?

After 1949, there were divisions within the Communist Party. The Party split over many things, including taking gradual versus dramatic steps on issues like how far to go in collectivising property and how doctrinaire to be about ridding institutions of people seen as tainted. Mao was impatient and impulsive. He wanted to transform the country quickly. He had a utopian streak. He thought that just as the peasantry could lead a revolution, despite Marx considering them a reactionary class, you didn't have to stick to the Soviet Union's path of moving slowly to socialism and then to communism. He didn't just want China to gradually catch up with Western powers but to leapfrog forward. He wanted its steel production to match Britain's—fast—and harvests to grow quickly. He thought that guided by the right ideology—meaning his revamped version of Marxism—and with people devoted to a mission, the Chinese could do things that others thought impossible.

The Great Leap Forward was the result of all this, a campaign to ratchet up industrial and agricultural production launched in 1958 that led to years of mass starvation. What went wrong? The central authorities set unrealistic targets for things like steel production that villagers could only meet by turning in their farming implements and having them put in furnaces and melted into useless pieces of metal. Crops were planted too close together and instead of leading to bumper harvests, this led to terrible ones. Simultaneously, local officials were afraid of being punished for failure, as failure would be seen as a sign of ideological impurity or lack of faith in Mao. Submitting misleadingly positive reports became a survival mechanism. People below Mao at all levels feared his wrath and tried to keep his always considerable ego inflated. This meant generally opting for a "full speed ahead" attitude rather than suggesting moderation or questioning his approach. There was bad weather, too, but that was only a small part of what led to tens of millions of people being reduced to eating bark and in many cases starving to death. It was a horrific period of suffering that only began to ease in the early 1960s.

The shift back toward a more normal course of development finally came when some of the respected elders in the Communist Party managed to sideline Mao a little. They got pragmatic people in to check Mao's excesses and introduce more realistic goals. It was a temporary victory for moderate voices in the struggle at the top between people who were more gradualist and those who were more ambitious and sided with Mao. The key players in these struggles were veterans of the Long March and other hallowed Party events, but none had as much charisma as Mao. He was not the only one whose personal history earned him respect within the Communist Party, but only he was the object of intense devotion. And it was this total respect for Mao and the blind faith his followers had in him that led to the catastrophe of the Great Leap Forward.

The Cultural Revolution

What exactly was the Cultural Revolution all about? What happened? When did it start and when did it end?

The Cultural Revolution was the most important event between the Great Leap Forward famine in the 1950s and Deng Xiaoping's rise to the top spot in the late 1970s.

Let's begin with how it started. The most important opening act of the Cultural Revolution came when groups of starry-eyed, enthusiastic but naïve young radicals, known as Red Guards, streamed into Tiananmen Square. They gathered there first in May of 1966 and kept coming back into that giant plaza. They came, sometimes a million at a time, to see Mao, the ageing leader they worshipped. He had been encouraging them to lash out against his real and imagined enemies, and that's what they did: first via wall posters and then by means of physical assaults and rituals of humiliation. After the horrible famine caused by his misguided Great Leap Forward policies, other leaders of the Communist Party, including Deng Xiaoping, had moved to sideline Mao and get the Revolution back onto the more pragmatic road toward nation-building and development it had been following in the mid-1950s. Mao, who at this stage in his life could be seen most charitably as a dreamer in a hurry, or less charitably and probably more accurately as a chaos-loving megalomaniac, was determined to shift the Party back onto a more utopian and fast-moving track. And to get back into the driver's seat. He saw the Red Guards as a loyalist militia he could use to get back in control—and get even.

Mao called for these loyalist youths and other true believers to carry out a "Great Proletarian Cultural Revolution". The idea was that a *cultural* revolution that would change the way people thought and behaved was needed to complete the work of the *political* revolution of 1949. That had failed, he claimed, to rid the country of "feudal" habits and "bourgeois" beliefs. China would be stuck in a bad situation, he argued, without shaking things up.

In the months following the first pro-Mao rallies of mid-1966, Red Guard bands and rival groups, whose members claimed to be even truer interpreters of the Chairman's wishes, launched attack after attack upon each other. They also lashed out against an ever-widening circle of individuals whose allegiances, actions, or even just ancestry left them open to charges of being "capitalist roaders", defenders of Soviet revisionism, and "counterrevolutionaries". In their eyes, those found in that circle were undeserving of humane treatment.

Eventually, those bullied, humiliated, and sometimes beaten to death or driven to suicide would include many former allies and protégés of the Chairman. Deng and Mao's one-time heir apparent Liu Shaoqi and other Party luminaries became targets, and so did members of their families and leading artists, academics, and authors as well as ordinary folks. Some of the targets of the Red Guards were hounded to death, like the great Lao She, author of the acclaimed novel *Rickshaw*. Others were badly wounded or left traumatised. One of Deng's sons, who later pushed for better treatment of the disabled, was put on that path by the injuries he sustained during the early days of the Cultural Revolution.

By the late 1960s, even Mao, lover of upheaval that he was, felt things had gone too far. He proclaimed the Cultural Revolution a success and called in troops to restore order.

In a convenient way, Chinese accounts of the Cultural Revolution turn Mao's wife and three of her allies—the "Gang of Four"—into scapegoats for all the bad things that happened between 1966 and 1976, the so-called decade of turmoil. After Mao's death, they were tried and convicted of trying to undermine the

Party. Punishing the Gang of Four and rehabilitating the reputations of many of their rivals was intended to bury the legacy of the Cultural Revolution.

There are a lot of features of the Cultural Revolution, though, that there is no consensus about from inside or outside of China. There is disagreement about causes, characteristics, and even very basic chronology, especially after Mao proclaimed that it was over. Was it triggered only by top-down directives and signals or also by bottom-up grievances and hatred? Is it best likened to the Terror of the French Revolution, Stalin's purges, the Holocaust, or a combination of all these events? Did it last for three years—from the formation of the Red Guards in 1966 until the army took control in 1969—or was it just one phase of the Cultural Revolution? There are those who insist it did not end until Mao's death in 1976 or even Deng's rise and launch of economic reforms in 1979. This suggests just some of the main lines of disagreement that are worth keeping in mind when thinking about that tumultuous time in Chinese history.

Most foreign analysts like me agree about the basic chronology of the Cultural Revolution, that it started in 1966 and ended in 1969. We also believe that to understand contemporary Chinese politics, it is crucial to keep the Cultural Revolution in mind. This is partly because the country's current generation of leaders, including Xi Jinping, grew up as that tumultuous event was underway, and what they and their siblings and parents experienced during it—as victims, perpetrators, or often as both victims *and* perpetrators—has inevitably left important marks on their psyches and worldviews. And a rare point that both Deng and his critics in the 1980s and Xi and his critics now have all agreed on is that another Cultural Revolution would be a bad thing.

Mao's Legacy

How is Mao remembered in contemporary China—and how has Xi Jinping reshaped that memory?

There is no getting away from Mao being a complicated and sometimes contradictory figure, which is in part why his legacy is open to varied interpretations and uses. He was both anti-intellectual and an intellectual, but with an earthy Hunan accent (an artefact of his growing up in the countryside) that was hard for many in China to understand. He liked to write poetry, was proud of his calligraphy and fashioned himself as a scholarly type, but he also liked to be seen as someone with peasant roots (though his family owned land and he went to an elite university) who was critical of intellectuals and carried out campaigns against them.

Before Xi Jinping, there was an assessment of Mao as having been 70 per cent right, 30 per cent wrong.

That idea of a mostly good but partly bad leader was formally put forward in a document in the early 1980s.

But Xi has had a different way of talking about this. He's talked about the first 30 years of the People's Republic of China and the second 30 years as two major periods, and said that we should not use the successes of one to criticise the other. That is, we need to see where we are today as benefiting from both periods. This implies that he is leading China into a third era. The second 30 years would have ended in 2009, which was around the time his status as heir apparent, destined to take power as General Secretary in 2012, became clear. Until Xi took power, the official line on Mao's legacy was that the 30 per cent of mistakes occurred during the Chairman's final years, from the Great Leap Forward to 1976, and then things got back on track during the reform era that got underway in 1979. Xi does not say that the reform era is in the past, but he suggests that in many ways he sees China now in a post-reform era, a golden age that builds on the accomplishments of both Mao and Deng.

In the old 70/30 idea about the Chairman, the period lasting from the Long March to the early 1950s is seen as belonging in the mostly good part. Xi accepts that but goes further than others before him in extolling such things. This is where his celebrating Mao's handling of the Korean War fits in. He says, in effect, "Look, you had all these different forces of the more developed world fighting on one side, and that war did not end in a defeat for North Korea and for the Chinese side." So Xi wants to be seen as an inheritor of Mao, a continuer of one side of the Mao legacy—not the Mao who liked to stir things up, not the Mao who believed in mobilising youth on the streets, not the Mao who let things get out of control, but the Mao who was responsible for strengthening the nation.

It is interesting that the Foreign Ministry, trying to stay in step with Xi, has been replaying a speech Mao gave in 1953 about standing up to the West in the Korean War. There is a timeliness to this, as the name of one mass campaign of the early Mao era was "Resist America, Support Korea". Mao wanted the war to be seen not as China working in its self-interest, but as the country he led siding with the underdogs against the hegemons, the US being the most important of those. It was part of Mao's desire to see China as representing the Third World and the countries that had felt the brunt of Western and Japanese imperialism. Xi wants to focus on the 1953 speech that depicted America as a symbol of imperialism. This imagery has resonance today. He wants to present the current pushback not only as protecting his country's economy but also as part of an international effort to resist a powerful America.

POLITICS & POWER

Tiananmen Square

You have studied a lot of student protests throughout Chinese history and throughout history in general. What happened in Tiananmen Square?

In 1989 a massive protest movement took place which culminated in a massacre near Tiananmen Square, a huge square in the centre of Beijing. The story of what happened is largely suppressed within China and largely misunderstood outside China, in part because it happened around the same time that communism was unravelling and ending in the former Soviet bloc. The China story, which had its own dynamic, is too often conflated with what was going on nearly simultaneously in other places under communist rule. One of the key things to know about the protests in 1989 was that they were an effort to get the Communist Party in China to do a better job of living up to its own stated ideals, and to try to support the trend within the Party toward liberalising and opening up that had taken shape after Mao's death. It was not an effort to end communist rule, which was the goal of Soviet bloc protests in the 1980s.

I wasn't in China in 1989 but was there three years earlier when there were some warm-up protests for Tiananmen, and among that whole generation there was frustration. Students felt that Deng and company were talking a big game on reform and opening up but what they were delivering was a half-hearted version of those things. The Party was saying, "We believe in reforming and opening up, we need to liberalise, we need to give people more control of their fate". But the students felt that this was being done more effectively in the economic realm than in the political one, and that there were a lot of partial gestures that suggested the Party needed to move in that direction.

It'll seem like a very trivial thing, but I want to talk about a rock concert to illustrate this. I was in Shanghai in 1986 studying the history of student protests when students began protesting. Here was the real thing—demonstrations on campuses and marches from there into the heart of the city. This was the first time that students had been really on the streets in significant numbers since the Cultural Revolution, but unlike then they weren't expressing fervent loyalty to the top leader. The students were inspired by calls for democracy and discussion of democracy by physicist Fang Lizhi, a liberal intellectual who was sometimes called the Chinese Sakharov.

But one of the things that riled up students in Shanghai, where some of the most intense protests took place that year, was frustration about a rock concert given by Jan and Dean, an American surf rock band that was like the Beach Boys, only not as big. They were touring China. It was the first time in Shanghai that there'd been a rock concert, and Jan and Dean were only the second rock group to make it to any part of China. The students were really excited about this because it fit in with what they thought the Communist Party was moving toward: letting them be more part of the world. For them, that meant being more in step with pop culture around the world. During the concert, some students got up to dance because they thought that's what you were supposed to do at a rock concert, but the security guards made them sit down. And for the students in Shanghai, this symbolised the feint toward openness that really didn't have any follow-through; we're going to give you rock concerts, but we won't let you dance.

So, then, in 1989, the protests restarted, and there were a variety of reasons why they could restart. A space opened up for them due to an unexpected event in April of that year—the death of Hu Yaobang, an official who was associated with the reformist and liberalising group within the Chinese Communist Party. Hu, who had once been Deng's expected successor, died a member of government, even though he had been stripped of high office in 1987 (due partly to his having taken a fairly light stance toward the protests that began the previous year), so there had to be a funeral for him. The students took advantage of the commemorations of his death by putting up posters that basically said the wrong people were dying. Hu was younger than some of the more conservative members of the Party. They said, "So some people are dying too young, some people don't seem like they're ever going to die." This was April 1989.

What did the government do?

The government tried to get the protest to stop quickly, and they used the same techniques they had in 1986. An editorial in *People's Daily* said, "This is creating chaos", which is a coded term for the Cultural Revolution. Unlike 1986, this time the students didn't return to the classrooms, they kept up the protests. "No, we're just trying to show our patriotism", they were saying. "We believe that there's too much corruption and nepotism. There's not enough support for the more liberalising wing within the Party."

And there was a lot of frustration at this point, especially economic resentment. The economy was improving because of the reforms, but it seemed to many that only people with good government connections were getting rich. There was a sense of unfairness among the students but among workers too.

There were protests not just at Tiananmen Square but in plazas all around the country. It was in part an anti-corruption and anti-nepotism movement, in part a call for more democracy, for more freedom of speech. You can say it was something of a counterculture youth movement. There were rock concerts in the square. Cui Jian, the most popular rock musician, came to the square and played on a makeshift stage set up by the students.

There was a kind of disjuncture as well as conjuncture in 1989. Yes, there were protests in many places under Communist Party rule. The ones in China, though, were not about ending that rule. It also seemed for a time as though there was a possibility that somehow the protests would bring about a course shift without altering the whole system, especially when the protests continued for weeks and grew bigger. There was an internal struggle within the Communist Party leadership, but clearly the people who were more politically conservative were getting the upper hand. And there were signals that the protests were not going to be tolerated. But the students stayed and students from around the country kept pouring into Beijing to join them. The newcomers didn't want the movement to end when they had just arrived.

Then workers started joining the movement as well and formed an independent labour union. And that really concerned Party leaders. They might put up with students letting off steam, but they knew from past experiences, including struggles that helped bring their party to power, that sometimes student protests might lead to members of other social classes joining them because they look up to students as potential intellectual leaders of the country. And admiration for scholars made the situation combustible.

There is a longstanding tradition in China, going back to the start of the 20th century, of students as a potential vanguard, a group whose activism in the name of patriotism brings other groups out. So once there were labour activists joining the movement, then troops were called in. The massacre near Tiananmen Square began in the middle of the night of June 3rd and continued on June 4th. The army just swept in and the tanks rolled in. While the tanks caused some harm, mostly it was soldiers firing automatic weapons that led to deaths and injuries. There were a lot of deaths, though we don't know exactly how many. Some of those killed were students, many were bystanders and workers who had come out to protest, and a few were soldiers who were burned alive in their vehicles, though crowds only attacked them after the shooting of unarmed civilians began. On June 5, the tanks were still on the streets, and that's when the famous photograph was taken, showing a man standing in front of a tank with other tanks in a line behind it. That's a banned image within China. And I really think the reason why it's considered so toxic by the regime is because it just shows the People's Liberation Army looking like an invading force. The People's Liberation Army is supposed to be the organization that protects the Chinese populace from foreign aggression, and there they were acting like conquerors.

The 'Tank Man'

The man that stood in front of the row of tanks in Tiananmen Square. What do we know about him? What do you think about the symbolism?

It's an amazing symbol. He's on this boulevard near the square with this long line of tanks, and it's unquestionably an act of incredible bravery. One interesting thing that is sometimes forgotten is that in the end, after the lead tank has slowly swerved back and forth and then stopped, he climbs up on the tank. And the Chinese Communist Party initially showed video of this and said, "Look, the Western press is talking about how vicious we were, but what restraint the driver of that tank showed! Look at this. He wasn't mowed down." And the Party initially tried to spin the whole story of Tiananmen in a way that made the soldiers the heroes and the students the villains.

"The students were out of control", this line claimed. "Everybody should remember what happened during the Cultural Revolution, and the army showed restraint, and some were burned to death for their patriotism". It was only after the massacre began that people got outraged and attacked the soldiers, but through selective use of footage, the Communist Party could say, "The heroes, the martyrs, were these soldiers".

They tried, for the first months after the bloodshed, to get this narrative to stick. They talked about Tiananmen a lot. They even showed images of the Tank Man. The problem for the Party was that lots of people around Beijing had seen what happened and knew that, in fact, the soldiers had fired on unarmed civilians first. And there had been many people, as many as thousands, who were just mowed down. Many people knew somebody who had been killed, and they knew that those people had not deserved to die. So that story just didn't stick.

And then the official handling of the story changed. There was a shift to trying to suppress discussion of the event and particularly to repress the image of the man in front of the line of tanks. Whatever the tanks did to him, the main takeaway from it would be that there were lines of tanks in the city. The image showed a government that had lost the mandate to rule, and they really didn't want to have that image out in the world.

Do we know if he was a student?

He was almost certainly *not* a student. He's often described as a student, but he was probably a worker. It is a powerful, powerful image of bravery, but he was not the first tank man to be featured in a famous photograph. I brought up the idea of 1989 in China paralleling 1968 in Eastern and Central Europe. There was a very powerful photograph of a man baring his chest in front of a tank in Bratislava during the Prague Spring. That image is not so well known now in many parts of the world, but it was iconic, another image of great bravery. And in 1968 in Bratislava, the tanks that rolled in were Soviet tanks. That image was understood in part as saying, "Look at that patriot willing to risk his life in the face of an invasion."

Again, I think you have the People's Liberation Army looking like an invading force, and that's what the Chinese Communist Party in a sense can't deal with about the story of 1989. There is a story China's leaders could tell to defend taking a hard line on Tiananmen. They can say that what people should remember about 1989 is that in the wake of that year the Chinese economy boomed. Life got better in material terms for many people under its control. By contrast, in the Soviet bloc, the protests succeeded and after that the lot of many people living in that part of the world got worse in material terms. The move away from Communist Party rule was painful there and in the Soviet Union itself when things imploded in 1991. The Chinese authorities could focus on this and say that China's people should be happy to have avoided the difficulties of an unsettling transition, even if there was a crackdown in which people were killed.

The Party could make that kind of argument and it sometimes makes it in indirect ways. But it still doesn't want specific discussion of the massacre and works hard to keep that image of the man and the tanks from being shown. If this image appears, whatever else is being said about that time, what lingers is a vision of Beijing being invaded by the very force celebrated in official versions of history as the one that protects the Chinese people *against* invaders.

What do you think was going through that man's head? Was it a heroic statement? Was it a purely primal, guttural 'I've had enough'?

It's interesting to speculate, but we just don't know, because he was never able to be interviewed afterwards. But I think having patriotism be part of the picture is important, because one of the students' main demands was: "We want the authorities to acknowledge that our actions are patriotic, that our goals are to help, not harm, the country. We're not here to take China back into the Cultural Revolution. We're here to express our love for the country if it goes in the right way. So will you admit that?" If the Party had budged on that issue, the student movement might have completely wound down in May, and it actually was winding down partly due to exhaustion by early June. The Party didn't budge on that point.

I think the Chinese Communist Party learned something about the power of the image after 1989, because we saw this when there were protests in Hong Kong. The government on the mainland really wanted to tell a story there of crowds out of control. And initially in 2014, and again initially in 2019, there were very orderly crowds, and it had trouble with that story. So they tried very hard to ban images of peaceful protests until there were some incidents, as there almost always are, of violence by crowds, and then they showed those images over and over again.

They also worked very hard, when the Hong Kong protests began in the 2010s, to avoid any use of soldiers to repress them. It was all done by the police. The Western press was often saying, "Will this be another Tiananmen? Will there be a massacre, or will there be soldiers on the streets?" The movements in Hong Kong were suppressed without the use of shooting to kill on the streets. There was shooting to wound. There were bean bag rounds, rubber bullets, and tear gas used. There was even tear gas let fly inside subway stations in 2019.

And all these things are really brutalising, but they didn't make the kind of images that sear in the mind the way that the Tiananmen Tank Man image did, or the image of a young Vietnamese girl being burned by napalm that became an iconic image during the Vietnam War, did. Those images really have an extraordinary power, and I think the Chinese Communist Party is now aware of that. There are very few photographs allowed of the Xinjiang extralegal detention camps. There is an awareness of how much power a photograph of a certain type can have.

What do you think happened to the Tank Man?

I really don't know. He could have been killed not on that day but at some later point. He definitely disappeared. It's interesting because very often, figures are made an example of in one way or another. For example, Liu Xiaobo, the most famous Chinese political prisoner of recent times and a Nobel Peace Prize winner, was imprisoned and not allowed to get enough medical care, so he died earlier than he should have, even though he wasn't sentenced to death. But as for the Tank Man, there was never a trial, even one that everyone knew would end in a conviction.

And there's another figure like this who's disappeared. A couple of years ago, there was a lone man who put up a banner on a bridge, Sitong Bridge in Beijing. And it was extraordinary. It had denunciations of the direction Xi Jinping was taking the country. It criticised Covid policies, but also dictatorial rule. And the banner, somehow he managed to have it up and get it long enough to be filmed and to draw attention and for the film to circulate. Again, another image of the power of images. And he's disappeared, and there hasn't been a show trial or even a secret trial, and again, we don't know if he's still alive.

Xi Jinping

What role does Xi Jinping play in the increase in censorship and tightening of control in China today?

My own feeling, based on going to China from the mid-1990s till about 2018, was that until 2008 each trip felt like it had at least a bit more space for experimentation, for doing things that were not really part of the official order. There was more breathing room for religious expression of varied kinds, a wider range of foreign books being translated and published. I often thought of what a bartender said to me in China in 1996: *meiyou yundong shenme doukeyi*, which means "as long as there is no political movement involved, anything goes." It was not that China was becoming a liberal democracy, far from it. But people year by year seemed to feel less worried about what they were saying and what they were doing. That trend stopped about 2008, the year of the Olympics.

Since the Olympics and since the financial crisis right after that, which China came out of in good shape, the Chinese Communist Party has started to seem cockier and in a better position to exert itself with verve internationally and tighten up at home. Its leaders are still insecure, aware of how many communist party states have crumbled and how many organisations like the one they lead have been forced to share power. Still, this went side by side with a kind of bravado, before Xi rose and even more after he rose.

And Xi was already the designated successor by the time the tide shifted. By 2008, he was in line to take power after Hu Jintao and in charge of security for the Olympics. There were people outside of China who thought the Olympics might end up being a moment that led to loosening, to more opening up, because when Seoul hosted the Games there was a shift in South Korea toward being a less tightly controlled right-wing dictatorship and ultimately becoming a democracy. Some people were hoping the Olympics might move China that way, but it went in quite the opposite direction instead.

What do we know about the structure of the Communist Party leadership? How much power does Xi actually have?

James Palmer, who worked in Beijing as a journalist and now is an editor at *Foreign Policy*, wrote an important piece a few years ago. He said we should all really be straightforward about what a black box Chinese elite politics is. We should not try to pretend we know more than we do. I guess you could say that there are black box aspects to many countries in terms of top leaders, but the one in China has always been particularly hard to see into—and in Xi's day it has become even more opaque.

We did use to have more of a sense of these factions, which sometimes came down to different views of how much tinkering there should be with the economy. And they were also partly based on personalities and personal ties, networks associated with places, too. We did have a sense you could map out these kinds of rival power bases and things. But we have much less of a sense of that under Xi. It's very hard to know who is in and who is out and why, other than there being some continuity in a small group around him. We don't have a major defector who says, "Yeah, this is how Xi Jinping operates." We have Xi Jinping's self-presentation and a lot of things that are said about him in hagiographic works buttressing his personality cult, but neither gives us much insight into what's really going on.

We do know that early on there were some false expectations about him. Some people thought, "He's going to be a reformer, because his father was a liberalising figure." It didn't work out that way. He does seem to care about orderliness, we know that. We know he wants to present himself as a kind of scholarly figure in touch with China's classical era, the time of Confucius. We know he's a strong nationalist and a cultural nationalist as well as a political nationalist. But beyond that, we don't have that much of a sense of what makes him tick. We get little hints. There was a secret speech that leaked early in 2013 in which he talked about how the Soviet Union had collapsed because the leadership didn't pay enough attention to ideology. And he also said that none of the top leaders there were "manly enough" to keep control. That imagery fits in with the resurgence of patriarchy. I imagine if he and Putin ever have a heart-to-heart conversation, one thing they'd find to agree on is their distaste for Gorbachev. They share a feeling that Gorbachev made the wrong moves—in Xi's eyes letting a communist party collapse, in Putin's letting an empire collapse.

Each is haunted by a different ghost. For Putin, it is the loss of an empire and he's determined to rebuild it, by force. Xi is haunted by what happened to the Soviet Union's ruling party more than its territory, though he has his own territorial ambitions. No recent Chinese leader has wanted to see the diminishment of China's size on his watch. And the most impressive ones are considered those who, in contrast, extended its territory. Mao created a new country and brought Tibet into it. And then Deng Xiaoping brokered the deal that brought Hong Kong and Macau into the country in 1997 and 1999, respectively, though he died just before the British handed over Hong Kong.

You have the story, a very powerful story about the Chinese past, that the Chinese Communist Party makes a lot out of reversing a long trend. Between the mid-1800s and 1949, foreign powers bullied China and chipped away at the vast territory that the Qing emperors had previously ruled, and then the Communist Party got things back on track. Chiang Kai-shek, when he headed the Nationalist Party and was Mao's great rival, also made a lot out of the goal of reversing the trend toward China getting smaller. There is a powerfully entrenched notion that there was a "century of humiliation" lasting from the 1840s until the middle of the 1940s. Chiang claimed he could regain China's momentum and make it a great power again, and he did do things like gain the country a seat on the UN Security Council as one of the victorious Allied powers in the Second World War. Before long, though, Mao and his Red Army had driven the Nationalists off the mainland and onto Taiwan.

There is definitely a basis for this story of diminishment and then resurgence. Beginning in the middle of the 19th century, China, which had been one of the richest countries in the world and clearly the most powerful one in its region, did get laid low, bullied, and nibbled away at by foreign powers, with even Japan joining Western powers in this process. It's important to realise there are elements of that story that are very true. There are also, though, exaggerations and false claims. Tibet was not always part of China. Xinjiang's very name means "new frontier", a sign that it was not part of China, really, until the Qing conquered it and brought it into their empire. And the very use of the word "China" to refer to the realm governed by different ruling groups over the course of millennia is misleading. There were different empires of radically different sizes between the First Emperor of the Qin and the Last Emperor of the Qing. And when recent leaders have made moves seen as "reclaiming" lost territory, moving China back toward being the shape some imagine it has always been, they are often really playing fast and loose with history. There were lots of periods when Taiwan was not ruled by any power on the mainland. Even with Hong Kong, which is described by Beijing as being "returned to Chinese rule" in 1997, things are complicated. There was no port metropolis of Hong Kong when Hong Kong was ceded to the British by the Qing at the end of the First Opium War, which lasted from 1839 to 1842. It consisted of a great harbour and some small communities at the edge of, and not fully incorporated into, the Qing Empire. And that Qing Empire was ruled by Manchus, not by a Chinese royal family.

Still, myths are important. It is important that leaders from Chiang and Mao on have been insisting that they will not be the ones who let "China" shrink or get less influential globally. From 1949 on, the Communist Party's claim to legitimacy has been rooted partly in the idea that the reason it deserves to rule is that it can reassert China's place in the world.

Taiwan

How important is Taiwan to China?

I don't think you can talk about Beijing and Taiwan without considering the fate of Hong Kong. The futures of Hong Kong and Taiwan are intertwined. In 1984, a deal was struck between London and Beijing over what would happen to Hong Kong. Hong Kong Island became a British colony at the end of the First Opium War. And then the Kowloon Peninsula, near there, became a British colony in 1860 after the Second Opium War. But then there was a large amount of territory of what we now think of as Hong Kong, called the New Territories, that came under British control in 1898 but was not a colony. It was a 99-year lease.

So, 1997 was the expiry date for the lease of this large amount of territory of what we now think of as

Hong Kong. It's a large amount of territory that the rest of Hong Kong, Hong Kong Island and Kowloon, depends on for energy, water, and food. It would've been very hard to just transfer those parts to the People's Republic of China. A deal was needed to determine what would happen in 1997. And the deal was about transferring sovereignty over all of Hong Kong, all these parts, to the People's Republic of China. And I carefully say transfer sovereignty, not give it back to the People's Republic of China, because it never belonged to the People's Republic of China. The Qing Empire was a different country, a different state.

And the deal that was struck was that the London side wanted to do something to protect the interests of the people there. And remember, this is not what usually happens to colonies. Colonies usually go from being part of an empire to being self-governing places. And because of that, the Chinese representative to the UN insisted that Hong Kong was not a colony and that Macau was not a colony, even though it was part of the Portuguese Empire, because then the two port cities would have to be decolonised and become independent at some point. Anyway, there was an understanding that something would have to happen in 1997, and London wanted some protection for the people in Hong Kong, who they knew were living in a very different way from people who lived under Communist Party rule. There was a different kind of rule of law. There wasn't democracy, but there was some degree of input in governance.

In the days of British colonial rule, the most powerful person in Hong Kong was appointed by London. After 1997, the most powerful person would probably have to be somebody who could work with Beijing. But in this negotiation, an idea emerged called "One Country, Two Systems". The idea was that Hong Kong would become part of the People's Republic of China in diplomatic terms. It wouldn't have its own military. But it would keep its own system for 50 years, from 1997 until 2047. There was a tension from the beginning over what that other "system" meant, what were going to be the realms of life that would stay separate. Everybody agreed it would need to have a different economic system. It had capitalism, so people agreed on that. But there was tension from the start over, well, what about legal matters? What about political, cultural and other things? And one thing written into this deal was that over time Hong Kong people would govern Hong Kong. Again, there was room for different views. Beijing thought what mattered was that a Chinese person would govern Hong Kong, but that it would have to be a Chinese person with deep ties to Hong Kong and who Beijing would play a role in choosing, to ensure they would see things Beijing's way.

How is this relevant to Taiwan?

In 1984, as Beijing was coming up with this plan jointly with the British, with Hong Kong people largely sidelined in the whole process, the Chinese Communist Party promoted the idea of "One Country, Two Systems". This arrangement is something people in Taiwan should pay attention to, because it could provide a model for what could happen in the future for them if they are absorbed into the People's Republic of China. Beijing said, "Hey, people in Taiwan, watch what happens to Hong Kong after 1997, and think about it as a model for what could happen with you", saying, "watch how smoothly it will go." Over time, people in Hong Kong started saying, "Well wait, Beijing keeps sort of nibbling away, chipping away at these things that make us separate", and especially after 2008, it seemed clear Beijing wanted the only "system" that was different to be the economic one.

There were reasons why Beijing went especially light on Hong Kong in the immediate aftermath of 1997. Beijing wanted to enter the World Trade Organization and it wanted to host the Olympics. A big move against Hong Kong, which might have been seen internationally as Beijing reneging on its word, could have endangered those things. Also at that point, the PRC was heavily dependent on Hong Kong economically. Because I'm a university person, I think about another factor too, which was the reputation of academic institutions on different sides of the border. In 1997 when Hong Kong became part of the People's Republic of China, Hong Kong universities became the first in the country to be considered world-class. The University of Hong Kong and the Chinese University of Hong Kong were highly rated institutions. And at that point, Peking University and Tsinghua were not yet considered world-class institutions, because they didn't have the kind of academic freedom and strengths in the humanities and social sciences that at that point were needed to get a high rating globally.

Over time, that difference started to go away, in part because global ratings of universities stopped factoring in academic freedom as importantly. Beijing universities ultimately surpassed Hong Kong ones, due partly to the money poured into their labs.

Beginning in the early 2010s, you started to have protests in Hong Kong pushing back against mainlandisation and defending a more robust rather than limited view of the "systems" part of "One Country, Two Systems". You also started having the authorities clamp down on things, supporting the view of the "systems" part not meaning much. Hong Kong protesters then put up a banner in 2014 that reached out to Taiwan's populace. At the time, Beijing was holding the line against Hong Kong people demanding real elections to choose the Chief Executive of their city. There was a popular vote held for that post, but only people who Beijing approved of could run, so it was more a *selection* than an *election*. The banner Hong Kong activists put up said in effect, "Hey, Taiwan, look at Hong Kong and be afraid. Hong Kong's today could be your tomorrow." This was putting a radical spin on the way Beijing talked in the mid-1980s about how "One Country,

Two Systems" could be a model for Taiwan. "Yeah, Taiwan. You should watch what happens here"—that's what the banner suggested. It had the phrase "Taiwan Beware" in English, and Chinese characters likening Hong Kong's present to Taiwan's future.

One way to think of Chinese leaders since 1949 is that Mao and those after him each wanted to be remembered as someone who made China bigger territorially than it had been. For Deng, that meant bringing in Hong Kong and Macau. Under Mao, Tibet. Tibet was offered something a little bit like "One Country, Two Systems" only to then be pulled tightly under Beijing's control. Isabel Hilton, who writes wonderfully about Tibet, has talked about the parallels between Tibet in the 1950s and Hong Kong recently. Some Hong Kong activists saw parallels as well. Tibet was supposed to go its own way as part of the People's Republic of China in the 1950s. And then by 1959, the centre got restless, tried to interfere more. Local people pushed back against it. And a workable structure—or a structure that seemed like it might work out somehow against all odds—exploded And the Dalai Lama went into exile. The Dalai Lama, who before that had thought maybe he and Mao could work together, that didn't work.

With Hong Kong, a new version of the experiment began and followed a similar path, though over a more protracted period. It was only in the 2010s, really, that a period like the 1950s in Tibet began. That was when it became clear that the centre was getting less patient, needed Hong Kong less, and that Hong Kong's people were feeling more and more that if they wanted to defend their special way of life, things would reach a now-or-never pushback moment. That came in 2019 with giant protests, and in 2020 Beijing imposed the National Security Law, which was like a form of martial law.

You could say that Deng Xiaoping oversaw the deal that got Hong Kong and Macau to become part of the People's Republic of China. He could point to that. Even though Deng died in February of 1997, before either territory became part of the country, he had been the one to strike the deal. Xi Jinping could argue that he was the one who truly finished the job of making Hong Kong fully a part of the People's Republic of China, doing away with the most troublesome, in Beijing's eyes, remaining forms of difference. A freer press, for example. That's now almost completely gone. Hong Kong fell fast from a high place to a low place in global rankings of press systems in the early 2020s. You could say that this makes it seem that Xi would see Hong Kong as a stepping stone toward Taiwan. Or you could say that in fully controlling Hong Kong and building up the South China Sea Islands, he has done things that allow him to claim he's been expanding Beijing's territorial reach. He can stake a claim to being a leader who made the country bigger.

Probably, to an extent, he would like Taiwan to become part of the People's Republic of China, which it has never been. Hong Kong being transformed, though, under his watch, to an extent, makes it less crucial that he do that. One thing that is clear is that the hope that Taiwan could become part of the PRC over time via uncontested, gradual absorption is gone. In part because of what's happened to places like Hong Kong, there's now a fiercer, stronger sense of Taiwanese identity than there was at an earlier point. Politicians who are more willing to try to negotiate some kind of tighter connection with the PRC can sometimes win elections, but these days they have more trouble than in the past because of this mood.

Invasion

What are the chances of military conflict over Taiwan in the coming decades and how can we avoid it?

It's one of these worrisome issues that there isn't an easy way to answer. I think experts who tell you they know how factors X, Y, and Z will determine whether or not there is going to be a military conflict are deluding themselves, probably. There are so many variables.

Talking to people in Taiwan while I'm there, and with people from Taiwan when I'm not, there are a couple things that are clear. One is that daily life in Taiwan is not people waking up each morning and living through the day obsessing over being in a perilous predicament. That is, life goes on and a lot of people feel very fortunate to be in Taiwan. There are many reasons why it seems like a great place to live. But at the same time there is an awareness of the precariousness of the situation. This meant there was a lot of concern, after the invasion of Ukraine, in seeing what the international response would be. There was a sense that Xi Jinping would be watching the response to Putin and deciding what he would do then.

Is there a loose historical notion that Taiwan should be part of China and therefore imminent action is not needed? Would Xi Jinping and the Communist Party accept that?

That loose idea has often been accepted. Chiang Kai-shek and Mao both thought that the mainland and Taiwan were somehow destined to be part of a single entity. It was just that, during that period, Mao thought, "How long until Taiwan is absorbed into the mainland?" while Chiang thought, "How long until I take over the mainland and it all becomes the Republic of China?" This is no longer something that any leader in Taiwan believes will happen. Things have not changed as dramatically on the mainland, so we can certainly say that if—a big if—there is ever an invasion, it won't be Taiwan doing the invading.

As if all this wasn't complicated enough, Taiwan isn't just one place or one island. There are islands that are part of the country that lie closer to the mainland than the big island where the capital city of Taipei is. Kinmen, for instance, is a part of Taiwan very close to Fujian province on the mainland. The

Communist Party has been trying to get people who are in Taiwan but closest to the mainland to think of themselves and the Fujian residents as part of a single zone. This has echoes for me of parallel moves that were made with Hong Kong in the 2010s. The idea of a Greater Bay Area, which included Hong Kong and cities just over the border, like Shenzhen, was pushed. I remember getting a "Greater Bay Area SIM Card" for my phone when I got to Hong Kong on one visit in the late 2010s. It promised me that I could use it to make calls in Hong Kong, Macau and Shenzhen, and it worked.

I don't know if moves like that to connect people across the strait will gain traction. It is just something worth keeping in mind. Similarly, if we remember Putin's invasion of Crimea more than a decade ago, we need to keep in mind the possibility of a Beijing military action that just tries to wrest control, initially, of a small island close to the mainland. Not that this will happen, just that it could.

CULTURE
&
CONTROL

Confucius

Tell us about Confucius, who lived some 2,500 years ago. Who was he exactly, and why does he still matter to China today?

First of all, we don't know that much about Confucius. He's from around the same time as figures like Socrates, and like with Socrates, we get a lot of what we know about him—or think we know about him—from what his followers said, things that were attributed to him and dialogues that were written afterwards. You can have a lot of fun placing Confucius and Socrates and other Axial Age thinkers side by side and contemplating what they had in common.

One thing that connects many of these thinkers in different places is that they were trying to make a case for why they should be able to educate the elite of the next generation. They promoted recipes for rule as well as visions of the good life, and they vied with one another for the right to serve their rulers as teachers or advisers. Confucius lived in a time when there were warring kingdoms in a territory that later became China, but none of these kingdoms were anywhere near as big as modern-day China.

What Confucius said was that there had been a period of great order in the past, before the chaos of the Warring States period, when the line between inferior and superior had once been clear—a major force in keeping disorder at bay. There was a kind of synergy between superior and inferior, he felt, that kept everything ticking along nicely. Confucius, who worked as an administrator in his home kingdom of Lu, thought that hierarchical relationships were a good thing as long as both sides in a hierarchical relationship knew what they owed the other and provided it. He emphasised things like the father and son relationship. The father deserved respect from the son, but owed the son care and benevolence, and things would be fine as long as both sides in the relationship held up their end. This was one of four crucial relationships, he asserted, and the other three were hierarchical as well.

One of the three relationships other than the father-son one was between husband and wife. It was unequal, he determined, with the husband owing his wife care and her owing him deference. He had comparable views of the relationship between an emperor and the officials who served him, and between elder brothers and younger brothers.

That last one is telling. In the West, we often think of the ties between siblings as quintessentially egalitarian relationships, and terms like brotherhood and sisterhood convey that. Even relationships between siblings got a hierarchical spin from Confucius. This reflects a tilt toward hierarchy in the Chinese language itself, as you cannot easily say "my sister" or "my brother" without designating whether you mean a sibling who is older or younger than you are. (This hierarchical tilt can be overcome, as the Communist Party does with its reference to ties between "comrades", conceived as equals. Some Confucian thinkers made a stab in that direction by proposing a fifth relationship, that between friend and friend, with each owing the other the same respect. Still, even in that modified form of Confucianism, having four out of five relationships involve superiors and inferiors remains striking.)

There was also a sense in which Confucius and other Chinese thinkers of the time connected the natural world to the supernatural world. In the Confucian view of politics and society, the emperor was supposed to serve Heaven—a kind of non-personified deity—as ministers were supposed to serve the emperor and sons their fathers. In fact, the emperor was referred to as the Son of Heaven.

Another important thing for Confucius was the call to study classical texts, which detailed how the sages of old behaved back when the world was stable and orderly. But Confucius thought that in his day, these codes of conduct, embodied in rituals of old, were not respected. As a result, society had been corrupted and was moving away from that sort of purity of the sages, and the relationships between inferior and superior were blurred. Confucianism, a richly varied tradition with many strands, has tended to be conservative or even backward-looking, though periodically some have called for reform while insisting on being true to Confucius. In its classic version, it wasn't arguing for progress, it was arguing for reclaiming a past golden age that had been lost. It also called for maintaining hierarchies, not overturning them. A lot of emphasis was put on emulating models of virtue. These included the sages of the period long before Confucius lived. But Confucius himself was described by his students as exemplary in his behaviour, too. The most famous early interpreter of Confucius's ideas, Mencius, was later similarly celebrated as exemplifying in his personal life as well as extolling in his writings such virtues as showing respect to one's parents, meeting the ideal of filiality, and caring for those needing and deserving support.

In all kinds of ways, Confucianism is irreconcilable with many ideas in Marxism and communism, which are all about struggle and all about a progressive view of history moving from one stage to the next to pursue an ideal of ultimate egalitarianism—even if communist societies have often ended up with new inequalities, including party elites enjoying great privilege. While

Confucianism looks to an ideal past, Marxism and communism look to an ideal future. Confucianism justifies hierarchies while Marxism and communism attack them. But both of these doctrines have strong legacies that continue to impact how many Chinese people think and feel today. This is a great contrast to point out. Another issue, I suppose, is that when the Communist Party was choosing a value system to promulgate, Confucianism was the safest and most useful. It sprouted and flourished on Chinese soil; it is an ethical system and not a religion, and it fosters convenient conservative precepts like obeying authority and striving for moral purity.

Education and Merit

China is said to place a high value on education and meritocracy. Can you explain Confucius's idea of education, and how much does it permeate the China of today?

There's an optimism to this idea, an optimism in the sense that people have the ability to learn to be good. And when exposed to exemplary figures from the past, they'll want to be like those exemplary figures. So it was a form of education through the of emulation of models and study of past figures and past texts that were exemplary. And it did have this idea, a relatively positive view of human nature and the sort of changeability of humans through education.

And I think that shows through in all kinds of things, including how the Chinese Communist Party has treated defeated enemies. There were lots of people killed by Mao and his allies, but there was often an idea that people could be remoulded, potentially. I'm struck by the fact that China is one of the few places where revolutionaries didn't kill the last monarch after establishing a republic. And the last emperor of the Qing, who was just a boy in 1911, was still alive when the People's Republic of China was founded. And, again, he was allowed to live. The idea was that, at least in principle, education, in this case re-education could redeem even a remnant member of a toppled royal family into a useful citizen. The notion that a onetime emperor could be turn into a comrade seems a carryover from the Confucian times.

And over time, this Confucian idea led to the creation of one of the early great civil service exams, and the idea that the bureaucracy should be run, not by people who were born into the right families, but by ones who had shown their ability to master these gruelling exams. And the exams could make or break your career, a bit like, at some points in the American past, passing a bar exam—an intensive process that could set you on the road to a good career. In China, you had the civil service exam tradition.

I think there is this kind of emphasis on education and on valuing scholarly pursuits, but then Chinese leaders throughout history, up to and including Mao and Xi Jinping, have also found scholars to be tremendously difficult to control. There's an ambivalence to it.

Does the meritocratic view still matter in China? The notion that if you work hard and you learn things, you will succeed, and if you haven't succeeded, that means you didn't work hard?

There's such a challenge in all these forms of meritocracy. You had the civil service exams, but if you had an especially good tutor, if you could afford a really good tutor, you had a better chance of passing the exams.

One thing that happened in imperial China was that families would pool together resources to try to help the brightest in their group to become part of the officialdom. And this kind of pooling together resources as a family was an important part of that structure. But there was always a tension in that—so what if you don't succeed?

Some of the leaders of rebellions against emperors were failed examination candidates.

Also, there was something built in that we can trace back not so much to Confucius himself, but to Mencius. As I mentioned, Mencius was the most important early interpreter of Confucius, and he promoted the idea of rule by heavenly mandate that can be seen as a crude justification for rebellion, even for a kind of democracy. He claimed that even though the emperor rules by the will of Heaven, if the man in the palace doesn't act like a true emperor, if he's not morally upstanding, then Heaven will remove its support from him. And then, if he's lost a divine mandate, there's no obligation for others to be loyal; they do not owe deference to a ruler who's not behaving like a true ruler. And this sort of justifies rebellion. And the idea is that if the rebellion isn't justified, Heaven will stop the ruler from being killed. But if Heaven has removed its support, then the rebellion will succeed, and then a new ruler will be justified in taking power. So it's an interesting sense that the universe in this Confucian view has a kind of moral dimension to it, but it's only when things actually happen that you see where the side of morality is.

The idea of meritocracy opens up any ruling order to criticism when there is a sense of unfairness about who's getting ahead and how the spoils are being divided, and this leads to a kind of outrage. Some of the biggest protests in China have been against this culture of nepotism, which really seems to subvert this whole idea of meritocracy.

Take the 1989 protests. Even though the protests were discussed in the Western press as a movement for democracy, a lot of the first posters that went up were criticisms of corruption and nepotism within the Communist Party. The belief that only those with connections were getting ahead led to intense outrage among the students. There was a special anger reserved for nepotism because of that meritocratic ideal.

Modern Censorship

How much censorship is there in modern-day China?

There's a lot of censorship. In one of my favourite books about Chinese censorship, Margaret Roberts's *Censored*, the author, a political scientist, talks about how there are three different ways that the government can control stories. She refers to the three Fs—fear, friction, and flooding—and she says they're all important, and I think this is true not just of China but in other countries too. She says there's fear, which is generated by direct censorship. The government creates a situation in which people worry about what will happen to them if they use certain taboo terms. Then there's friction. This means that the authorities make it harder for people to get information that they don't want people to get. Even though they know that some people will access information that contradicts official line, they create a situation in which that the first answers people will get through a search will be an answer that supports rather than challenges the Communist Party's position on a topic.

There were versions of friction before the age of the internet, with some "banned" books, for example, being published but in limited circulation, so you had to work hard to get access to them. They were supposedly just for the central elite, but others could find ways to buy them; it just wasn't easy. With the rise of the internet in the very late 1990s and into the 2000s, the friction strategy became a more important method of controlling information.

As for flooding, a good way to think about this is to consider propaganda drives as being like incredibly big advertising campaigns. The airwaves are filled with stories and billboard space is covered with images and ideas that reinforce a particular view, in this case not of a product to buy but a way of thinking about China's past, present, and future that conforms to a particular worldview. People just got used to hearing and seeing certain kinds of ideas, and more recently the internet has been full of stories, pictures and videos that encourage those who spend time online to think about politics, society and China's strengths, as well as the weaknesses and dangers of other places and systems, in a certain way.

A lot of tech-savvy or globally minded, tapped-in Chinese people will use a VPN to jump over the firewall. But it takes work and time to do that.

The internet moves more slowly. You have to keep updating your VPN. The authorities create friction so that most people will give up rather than keep trying to get beyond official versions of stories. And the impact of the friction is even greater due to flooding—constant passive exposure to versions of the news and stories that the authorities want the people to believe. All those exist and are in operation at the same time.

Does anything escape the censors?

I'm always interested in things that you would expect to be censored that aren't censored. You can read all sorts of things in China about totalitarianism. You can read Hannah Arendt's book on totalitarianism. You're not supposed to be able to read that in a totalitarian state or a dictatorial state, but it's not specifically about China. And so censorship is most restrictive when it concerns text that focus on China. Material about the private lives and wealth of leaders of the Chinese Communist Party and about certain sensitive subject is intensively censored. But ideas conveyed through allegory, through imagining a place that looks a lot like a Communist Party-ruled state, are often tolerated.

There are texts that were banned up until the very last period of Gorbachev's rule, banned throughout nearly the whole history of the Soviet Union, that have been available in Chinese bookshops for decades. You can buy *Nineteen Eighty-Four* in Shanghai or

Chengdu or Beijing. You've been able to since 1985. It's a book that is not specifically about China. And actually, for some people living in the PRC in the mid-1980s who focused on the part of *Nineteen Eighty-Four* depicting the "Two Minutes Hate", those rituals of denunciation seemed like they were about the country's Mao era past, not its reform era present.

By the time the 1990s came around, some aspects of how life in the world of *Nineteen Eighty-Four* was portrayed seemed even further removed from life in contemporary China. The book depicts bleak time of a of scarcity in a place where people just aren't having fun. Some people would read *Nineteen Eighty-Four* and say, "Look, this is about a world like ours. We, too, are trapped in a Big Brother state." But others said, "Well, that has some similarities to China now, but Orwell wasn't talking about a country much like ours. Look, we've got supermarkets. We've got McDonald's. We've got fast trains. We're living so much better in some ways than our grandparents did, and this isn't like that bleak world he was imagining."

Censorship is not a static thing, of course. It is possible that if *Nineteen Eighty-Four* were not already available for sale, no publisher would be able to get permission to bring out an edition of it in Xi's time. There are ways that more of Orwell's depiction of dystopia is becoming a closer fit to China again. There are no Two Minutes Hate-like rituals but personality cult rule is the norm again. The repression is particularly tight now in parts of the country, such as Tibet and Xinjiang, and there is a bleakness and paranoia to life there for many people. But at certain moments, such as during the rigidly enforced 2022 Shanghai Covid lockdown, *Nineteen Eighty-Four* gains relevance even in what are generally lightly controlled parts of China. I've argued before that there are aspects of China now that bring an earlier dystopian classic more to mind than *Nineteen Eighty-Four*: Aldous Huxley's *Brave New World*. In that vision of an autocratic future, usually seen as relating more to capitalism than communist party rule, the powers that be maintain control by manipulating desires and keeping people distracted more than by the technique of the boot-on-the-face Orwell described. I still think Huxley is worth keeping in mind when thinking about China, but we've seen more of the boot-on-the-face under Xi.

Journalism on the Edge

How difficult is it to operate in China as a foreign journalist today?

It's certainly gotten harder for journalists to operate in China. There is a sense in which now journalists look back to the late 1990s and early 2000s, feeling it was quite extraordinary what they could do back then. Foreign reporters I know and sometimes hung out with in China then would complain about the challenges they faced. They were followed a lot, sometimes hassled if they pushed too hard on specific sorts of stories. It was hard to get permission to go to some places. There were people who would only be quoted anonymously, people who wouldn't talk to them at all.

It was no picnic then, and yet, in retrospect, all of the reporters I know feel that it was a lot easier then than it is now. In every area I've referred to, things have gotten worse: more surveillance, fewer people willing to go on the record, you name it. There has also been a dramatic reduction in the size of newsrooms in China, and obtaining visas has become more torturous. More places and topics are treated as taboo, and more cases come up where you only get a short-term visa. The early Covid years were incredibly hard for foreign journalists, though some managed to do extraordinarily good reporting in adverse circumstances. And things haven't really bounced back fully since then. And as bad as things are for foreigners who report from China, those I know are especially concerned by how it keeps getting more dangerous for the Chinese colleagues they work with, as a concern about having your visa revoked and having to leave the country is less dire than being arrested, having your family members harassed and so on. Journalists who have foreign passports but are of Chinese descent also often face bigger risks than those who are not.

In terms of taboo topics, there are places, like Xinjiang and Tibet, and moments in history like Tiananmen that are touchy. There is also, much more than there was in the 1990s, an effort to make discussion of the lives of top leaders off-limits. I've thought sometimes that Xi Jinping seems to have *lèse-majesté* envy; he wants there to be a sense that reporting on him beyond his public speeches is dangerous.

Is it safe for journalists and folks who write books about China to travel to China?

A lot depends on who exactly you mean. Until recently at least, the people who were most vulnerable were people of Chinese descent. People originally from China who had gone abroad and come back, or even Chinese Americans travelling in China, faced special risks. There was a higher expectation that they should be on board. You had cases more than a decade ago. My friend Melissa Chan was kicked out early when she was working for *Al Jazeera* and reporting on Xinjiang. So that's one kind of person who was vulnerable because of this expectation that they should be somehow more loyal.

Another kind of person who is vulnerable, or in this case more likely to be blocked from China, is someone with close ties to people Beijing wants to silence. The Communist Party is particularly concerned about people from outside China who are amplifying the voices of people within China, or exiles from China who the government would like to sideline. The Dalai Lama, for example. You have had scholars who worked on Tibet and had connections to the Dalai Lama—they were people who would have had trouble going to the PRC for a long time. The same goes for scholars who worked on Xinjiang, especially but not exclusively those connected to Uyghurs. Some people hassled or denied visas have also been people who have been personally connected to Han Chinese dissidents or exiles and sought to to amplify the voices and translatd the works of these critics of the Communist Party.

As for me, I wrote critical op-eds about the Chinese Communist Party. I published them in some high-profile places. I've written a lot about Tiananmen and given talks about human rights issues. And yet I kept getting visas to go to China. I even testified before the Congressional-Executive Commission on China when it held a hearing to commemorate the Tiananmen events on the 25th anniversary of 1989, but I got a visa right after that. There is just something unpredictable and quirky about it. Now it might be different. Some of the expectations have been changed.

The unpredictability can lead to people being careful and holding back in various ways, especially if they have special reasons to want to keep going to China, from completing a long-term research project that depends on being in the country to having family members there. Whenever I was giving a public talk at a Chinese university, I was keenly aware of the potential consequences of bringing up some taboo topics. It was generally not because I was worried about my own safety, but because I didn't want to get someone who was hosting me in trouble. And you are never quite sure which previously unproblematic topic may become problematic. I was told in the mid-to-late 2010s that there was concern about a talk I was going to give on the Boxer Crisis of 1900. It had long been an unproblematic topic, but an online feud had broken out in which some people were criticising rivals for being "Boxer-like" in the sense of being too narrowly nationalistic to the point of being xenophobic. They were attacked in turn with a different term from 1900. Wasn't it better to be like a "Boxer", some posted, than to be Chinese yet in lambasting Boxerism act like a supporter of the "Eight Power Allied Forces", the international army of soldiers from around the world who invaded China in 1900? I gave my talk without incident. I had planned to stick mostly to the events of 1900 and was undecided about whether or not I would slip something in that touched lightly on the legacies of the Boxer Uprising and foreign invasion. When the time came for my presentation, realizing that dealing even in passing with contemporary debates that invoke 1900 might create problems for my host, I stuck completely to the past. This wasn't a dramatic case of self-censorship, since I made every point that I had planned to make without cutting any part of my prepared remarks, but it was an example of steering clear of a touchy topic out of deference for a Chinese colleague's situation. So I guess I did engage in a bit of self-censorship.

Life in the Margins

Is the story of communication in China then just a tale of censorship and control through distraction? Are there other things going on?

There is a *lot* more going on. The journalist Christina Larson wrote a wonderful article during her time in China in the 2010s that argued for thinking of the internet there as being not just worse in some respects than varieties not behind the Great Firewall but also better in others. It's common to note that some people in China use VPNs to "jump" over the Great Firewall and get access to what is being said in other places. When she wrote about being able to have the "best" as well as "worst" online experiences in China, though, she had something else in mind. If you went online to get news there were problems, but if you went in search of fun, entertainment, or food, it could be great. To give just one example, the restaurant reviewing apps were much better than Tripadvisor. You could find out which dishes were best at a diner on a particular night, which waiter to avoid. And there was a very lively book discussion site, like Goodreads only with more back-and-forth engagement.

Some things Larson said still hold true, from what I have heard from people who've been going back to China since Covid restrictions lifted. And some things still hold true that Kate Merkel-Hess and I flagged way back in 2008, like when it came to politics, there were uses of the internet that fit in nicely with government policies but were not exactly propaganda, such as describing acts of official corruption. Then, as now, there were campaigns to rein that in. There were also, we noted, instances where something that was not a "dissident" post moved a bit in that direction by highlighting something the government preferred to keep hidden but had opened the door to having it discussed. We illustrated this, since we were writing just before the first Beijing Olympics, by noting that there had been official reports about Olympic competitors from around the world having no reason to be worried about eating pork in China, since special pigs were being set aside for them that were fed organic diets and monitored. This led to sly commentaries that repeated the fact but added a comment about it making readers wonder what horrible things people consuming the meat of "normal" pigs were ingesting. This was also a time when there were a lot of reports about coal mine accidents. Suddenly, comments kept showing up in different forms on different blogs that were variations on the statement: "I'd rather be an Olympic pig than a man in a coal mine!"

Another thing we noted was that China wasn't always behind other places even when it came to trends and popular culture. You saw then, and still see now, stories about books and films that were popular in many places but that Chinese consumers couldn't access, or at least had to wait to read or see. We were writing when young people in many lands were eager to get their hands on new instalments of the Harry Potter series, and American fans sometimes had to wait for US releases of new books until a few months after British fans had read the UK edition. So we noted that during the dramatic build-up to the finale of the series, some young people in China had it better than their American counterparts. While waiting, they could read original online works that took the characters in the series in new directions. This was partly because of a loose adherence to international copyright conventions, but also because online fiction was quicker to take hold in China. When a new edition dropped in the UK, sometimes groups of fans in China, and this was before Google Translate, would crowdsource translation and get a Chinese version out very fast, as a communal act to aid their peers who had weaker English language skills. We also pointed out that while books based on blogs were being hailed as a publishing novelty in the West in 2008, works in this genre had been making bestseller lists in China since 2006.

One other aspect of the Chinese internet that fascinated me is the humorous play that goes on there. Some of it is political and some not, but the political versions that get around censorship, going back to that, are particularly interesting. I love an example related to feminist activism that I first learned about from Maura Cunningham. When the government got annoyed with feminist activists embracing the phrase #MeToo and banned it, Maura told me, some clever netizens began including images of rice bowls and bunnies in their commentaries. This is because the character for rice is pronounced *mi* in Mandarin while *tu* is the pronunciation for the character meaning rabbit.

The internet is still a place for humorous play, not just by wordplay but also by filling social media with images that are not obviously criticising the government but can easily be read that way. It can take censors time to scrub them away, and by the time they do, in a sense, the damage has been done in terms of poking holes in some of the Communist Party's efforts to present itself as above reproach and as having the interests of the people at heart. To ban things after that has happened can be to close the barn door after the horse has escaped.

A couple of years ago, for example, some Shanghai revellers had great fun with Halloween costumes. What did people do? Things like dressing up with objects on their heads that hid their faces and made them look like robots with surveillance cameras where eyes would normally be. Having a few people on Shanghai streets see people dressed like CCTV cameras wouldn't have been a big deal, but when images of those costumes and others that mocked official control zipped onto screens all over the place, it generated anxiety in Beijing. The next year the authorities banned celebrations of the holiday, but this just made them look foolish, so thin-skinned that they couldn't take a joke.

Epilogue: The Other China

What do you think China will look like 25 years from now? What are your hopes?

It's such a hard moment to be imagining these things. I've long wanted to see a return of China to this path toward a more open society. I wasn't one of the people who imagined that there would be this convergence of China and the US, with both becoming liberal democracies. But I'd love to see a return of China with more openness to diversity, more space for civil society. It's a hard time to even imagine that, because Hong Kong—which once represented that place—has been repressed and forced to fit into a mainland mould. It was amazing looking backward, rather than forward, that Hong Kong was able to stay as culturally vibrant and on such a different track as long as it did after 1997. It's extraordinary how much leeway was given to Hong Kong for a period, and how successful those civic movements were in keeping Hong Kong different from the mainland and keeping it special. No Communist Party-run country had ever had a city within it that had as free a press as Hong Kong had then, as much tolerance for protests. I would like to believe that someday the restricting of Hong Kong will be viewed by some within Beijing as a miscalculation.

Thinking about hope, I'd love to think that there was some way that a variety of things that exist in Taiwan could become broader norms, spread to the mainland. It's not that Taiwan's perfect, it has its own internal problems, but there are many really attractive things about it right now. So maybe a China that somehow became more like Taiwan in its post-martial-law days, with lots of elements that are in step with Chinese cultural traditions, yet in a decidedly post-Leninist phase. That would be something that we could think of more as a future to wish for.

I would like to see a reversal of what's happening today under Xi—the stifling of variety—what Geremie Barmé often refers to as the "Other China", one that is more cosmopolitan, more open. Barmé, an Australian scholar who now lives in New Zealand, insists that the people and sometimes institutions and places that exemplify this "Other China" should be seen as embracing a worldview that diverges sharply from that of the Chinese Communist Party. More than that, what exemplifies the "Other China" are modes of thinking that Beijing wants people inside the PRC and around the world to think of as "foreign", but that in fact are distinctively Chinese. They are just associated with a different sort of Chineseness than the officially endorsed one. "Other China" representatives can show up on the Chinese mainland in underground salons and places where people meet and talk in ways that challenge official lines. This "Other China" also flourished for a time in Hong Kong and flourishes now in Taiwan. It also comes to life outside of East Asia in bookshops in Thailand, Europe and the US that hold literary and political events of a sort that would be dangerous or impossible to stage in any part of the PRC now, even Hong Kong.

That's very hopeful. Do you have fears things might get worse?

Plenty of them. They are rooted partly in my concern with aspects of China, such as the powerful hold the Communist Party still has and the influence of decades of nationalistic propaganda, but right now, midway through 2025, they are being ratcheted up by concern about global trends. And by what the US government during Donald Trump's second term has been doing. I worry that the trend toward tightening we have seen inside of China will continue. But I also worry about the way the world has been spiralling in a dangerous direction. It is going toward being a place where strongmen and powerful countries feel there are not—and should not be—any guardrails to check their ambitions. This has implications for what Beijing will do internationally, and none of them are good. I worry about the declining power of international institutions and international norms.

At the moment I don't see any signs of a shift away from the current tightening phase in the PRC on the immediate horizon, and I also don't see any sign just now of the global autocratic wave cresting and crashing. I don't want to predict that something that would allow more oxygen for "Other China" expressions will happen any time soon, even if it is easy to get a sense of the desire for this in some discussions held secretly in real life in the PRC and in carefully worded, playful and coded online discussions. I also don't want to predict that a new international democratic wave that could have a positive impact on China is starting to build, even if there are a few hopeful signs on the horizon amid the disturbing ones, like South Korea's politicians and protesters blocking martial law last year and then making an impeachment stick. It's a dark time. But developments in Chinese history and in world history have surprised us before. There is no reason to assume that at some point, perhaps after the time of both Xi and Trump, they will surprise us again.

Selected Reading

What are some publications or other resources that can help busy people get a deeper understanding of topics you have brought up in your answers?

Let's begin with Xi Jinping. We are still waiting for a really satisfying readable biography of him. Some useful books have come out on his ideology and there's a notable biography of his father, who was a major figure in his own right and influenced the son in varied ways. We just don't yet have anything that is an accessible, engaging and lively read that gets at what makes him tick. While waiting for that book, there's a good eight-part podcast called *The Prince*, which Sue-Lin Wong did for the *Economist* in 2022. There's also a profile called "Born Red" that Evan Osnos wrote for the *New Yorker* back in 2015 that holds up well as an entry point for grappling with this figure.

On Mao, there are more satisfying and certainly more abundant choices. One of my personal favourites is a brief biography by Jonathan Spence, which presents Mao as a Lord of Misrule. Geremie Barmé's *Shades of Mao* is good on the Chairman's legacy. And for the international impact of Mao's ideas, I like Julia Lovell's *Maoism: A Global History* and Alexander Cook's edited collection on the many meanings around the world of the "Little Red Book", the iconic object that Red Guards waved at rallies that brought together snippets of Mao's writings.

A detailed but very readable survey of the Communist Party's history, which pays a lot of attention to Mao's life and political actions and also moves into the present, is Tony Saich's *From Rebel to Ruler*. And a good novel to read along with it is Yu Hua's *To Live*, which gives a feel for what it was like for an ordinary family to experience many episodes in Chinese history. The film adaption that Zhang Yimou directed is excellent, too.

The Great Leap Forward famine and the Cultural Revolution are topics that can be explored through works of fiction, films, and memoirs as well as books of non-fiction. On the Great Leap Forward, Yan Lianke's novel *The Four Books* is a searing and surreal treatment, and among the memoirs there is a powerful section on it in the memoir *An Innocent Life in Mao's China*. The definitive works on it to me are Yang Jisheng's *Tombstone* and Frank Dikötter's *Mao's Great Famine*.

None of those works on the Great Leap Forward are quick reads, but I'm glad to say there are two excellent short books, one new and the other old, that I can recommend on the Cultural Revolution. The former is *Bombard the Headquarters* by Linda Jaivin, author of *The Shortest History of China*, which I also like a lot. The latter is Rae Yang's *Spider Eaters*, a memoir that stands up really well. Those take you inside the Cultural Revolution itself, but when it comes to legacies of the event, Tania Branigan's recent prize-winning volume *Red Memory* is a good place to turn.

I've given shout-outs in my answers to some books I like on the way China has changed during Xi's time in power, especially in relation to censorship, but I want to mention three online resources for those topics. One is *China Digital Times*, which tracks censorship especially well. Another is *China Heritage*, put out by Geremie Barmé. Last but not least, there's *ChinaFile*, a publication of the Asia Society. It runs everything from deep dive reports to forums that have people with different views on topics weighing in with short posts.

The main force behind *ChinaFile* is Susan Jakes, who spent time as a journalist covering China for *Time* and then entered a graduate program in Chinese history before pivoting to work at the Asia Society. I collaborated with her on a collective blog called "The China Beat" that no longer exists, though its posts are stored in a digital archive housed at the University of Nebraska. The blog was launched in 2008 and was edited first by Kate Merkel-Hess and then by Maura Cunningham. Many people I've mentioned contributed to it, as have other talented writers ranging from Peter Hessler (author of *Oracle Bones*) to Lijia Zhang (author of *"Socialism is Great!": A Worker's Memoir of the NewChina*). Two others who wrote for "The China Beat" are Alec Ash, who now edits another important Asia Society venture, *China Books Review*, and Ian Johnson, who is one of the key people involved in a recently launched collective venture, the China Unofficial Archives, which is a major online repository of materials that challenge orthodox Communist Party views of the past and present. Johnson, one of the best journalists to ever report from Beijing, has written several works worth checking out, including *The Souls of China*, which is on religion.

Rana Mitter provides an excellent brief survey of the last century or so of Chinese history in *Modern China: A Very Short Introduction*. A good recent work to pair with that is Edward Wong's *At the Edge of Empire: A Family's Reckoning with China*, in which the *New York Times* reporter combines accounts of his father's experiences in various parts of the country, including Xinjiang, with his own travels to the same locales decades later. On Xinjiang specifically, I am a big fan of *Waiting to be Arrested at Night*, a poignant memoir by Tahrir Hamut Izgil, a Uyghur poet who watched many of his friends disappear into camps and lives in exile. It's available in an elegant translation by Joshua Freeman. On Hong Kong, Louisa Lim's *Indelible City* is a great read by someone who knows the metropolis and its history inside and out, and Ching Kwan Lee's new *Forever Hong Kong* is excellent on protests and issues of colonialism.

On Taiwan, well, it's having a moment in terms of new carefully researcher but reader-friendly publications in English. As a basic introduction, Lev Nachman and Jon Sullivan's *Taiwan: Contested Democracy Under Threat* covers a lot of ground succinctly and well. Chris Horton's *Ghost Nation: The Story of Taiwan and Its Struggle for Survival* is valuable, too. Also, Jeffrey Ngo, a Hong Kong activist turned exile and doctoral student at Georgetown, wrote a short piece I have recommended often, "The Island the Left Neglected", which ran in *Dissent* magazine. *New Bloom* is a Taiwan-based periodical I turn to a lot to keep up with events and cultural trends there.

Switching from what you can read to things to watch, my favourite feature films for shedding light on post-1949 China are Jia Zhangke's. All of them, as he's my favourite Chinese director. And the documentaries I rate highest, though admittedly I'm a bit biased since I've consulted on some of them, are by the Long Bow Group. *The Gate of Heavenly Peace* and *Morning Sun* stand out to me as major interpretive works on Tiananmen and the Red Guards. I also love the Long Bow Group'searlier *Small Happiness*, a film about women in a Chinese village. That was one I didn't have a hand in, but someone who did, historian Gail Hershatter, wrote a book that complements it well. It's *Women and China's Revolutions*, which provides a fresh overview of the last century and a half by placing issues of gender at the centre.

Other recommendations include *China in Ten Words*, by Yu Hua, memoir-infused meditations on key terms. *Dr. Bethune's Children* by Xue Yiwei, a talented Chinese writer long based in Canada who deserves to be better known globally. *Life, Liberty, and the Pursuit of the Dao: Ancient Chinese Thought in Modern American Life*, by Sam Crane, who is good to read on all things related to Confucius and how he is understood, misunderstood, used, and misused. And Megan Walsh's *The Subplot: What China is Reading and Why It Matters*, a short book published by Columbia Global Reports. *The Subplot* makes clear how much we miss about Chinese cultural life if we only focus on what *can't* be read in China.

JEFFREY WASSERSTROM is a Distinguished Professor of History at the University of California, Irvine, and a specialist on modern Chinese political culture. He is the author of *Vigil: Hong Kong on the Brink* and *China in the 21st Century: What Everyone Needs to Know*. A frequent contributor to the *New York Times*, *Guardian*, *TLS*, and *Atlantic*, he is one of the most widely respected Anglophone commentators on China today.